TECHNOLOGY IN ACTION

AIRCRAFT TECHNOLOGY

Mark Lambert

Titles in this series

Aircraft Technology

Car Technology

Spacecraft Technology

TV and Video Technology

Ship Technology

Train Technology

First published in 1989
Wayland (Publishers) Ltd
61 Western Road, Hove
East Sussex BN3 1JD, England

©Copyright 1989 Wayland (Publishers) Ltd

Edited by Jollands Editions
Designed by Alison Anholt-White

British Library Cataloguing in Publication Data
Lambert, Mark, *1946-*
Aircraft technology
1. Aircraft. Technological innovation, to 1986
I. Title. II. Series
629.133

ISBN 1-85210-784-7

Typeset by Direct Image Photosetting Limited, Sussex, England
Printed in Italy by G. Canale & C.S.p.A., Turin
Bound in France by A.G.M.

Front cover The French experimental combat aircraft, the Rafale. Equipped with advanced flight control systems, this aircraft will enter service in the 1990s.

Contents

The aeroplane is a true product of this century. In 1900, transport on sea and land was well established, but no one could then foresee that travel by air would soon be possible. The first successful powered aircraft did not take to the air until the Wright brothers flew their *Wright Flyer 1* in December 1903. In the next five years, the Wrights and other American and European pioneers made further flights in experimental aircraft of strange and varied designs. These first aircraft were powered by small internal combustion engines, a recent invention, and the flying surfaces were controlled by a simple system of wires, pulleys and levers.

In those early days of flight the aeroplane had no obvious role. Few people believed that the frail, unsafe machines of the pioneers would ever provide a serious means of transport, and little did they know how important aircraft would soon become. The early pilots were concerned only with getting their machines to take off and fly, an enormous challenge in itself.

By the First World War (1914–18), powered flight had become established. At first, aircraft were used by both sides for spotting enemy movements. These reconnaissance aircraft had to defend themselves and were armed with guns, resulting in dogfights and the beginning of air combat. Aeroplanes were also used for dropping bombs and, by the end of the war, both sides had developed a variety of large and small military aircraft.

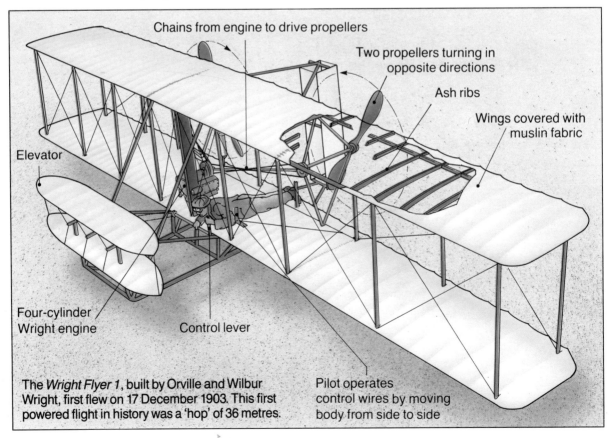

Chains from engine to drive propellers

Two propellers turning in opposite directions

Ash ribs

Wings covered with muslin fabric

Elevator

Four-cylinder Wright engine

Control lever

The *Wright Flyer 1*, built by Orville and Wilbur Wright, first flew on 17 December 1903. This first powered flight in history was a 'hop' of 36 metres.

Pilot operates control wires by moving body from side to side

Most human-powered aircraft fail to get off the ground because they lack the power to do so.

used for carrying mails, freight and also passengers. After the end of the Second World War (1939−45), the introduction of the jet engine and helicopters transformed the aircraft industry and the range of uses for aircraft increased still further.

Today, aircraft design undergoes constant changes and improvements as the result of rapid advances in a number of new technologies. These affect the design of engines and airframes, helped by the invention of new materials that are lighter and stronger than those used in the past. The modern electronics industry developed largely as the result of the need to find ever smaller and lighter components for spacecraft. Aviation electronics, avionics as it is called, and the use of computers, increase the safety and efficiency of all types of modern aircraft.

Between the wars, anything to do with flying and speed captured the public imagination. Throughout the world there were races, air shows and aerobatic displays. Aircraft were

The technology that has made the modern airliner possible has all been developed during this century. Aircraft design is changing and developing all the time.

An aircraft flying straight and level is being acted upon by four forces. Its **weight** acts downwards and is balanced by an upward force known as **lift**. The engines provide forward **thrust**, which balances the **drag**, the resistance caused as the aircraft forces its way through the air.

The all-important lift is generated in an aeroplane by the wings. These have a special shape known as an aerofoil, which in cross-section can be seen to have a curved upper surface and a flat undersurface. Air passing over the wing has further to travel over the top of the wing and has to travel faster. The pressure of the air immediately above the wing is therefore lower than the pressure of the air underneath and the wing is pushed upwards.

An important factor in maintaining lift is the angle of attack, that is, the angle at which the wing meets the air. Lift can be increased by increasing the angle of attack up to about 16°. Beyond this angle the air ceases to flow smoothly over the top of the wing and the lift is lost. At this point the aircraft is said to stall. It loses forward movement, becomes nose heavy and starts to dive. The pilot loses control until lift can be established again.

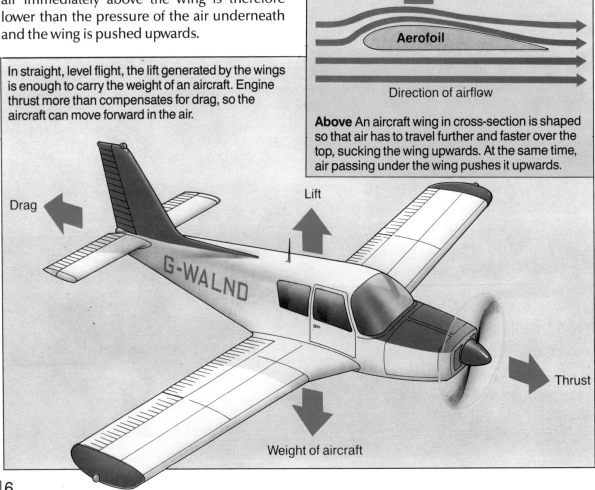

Lift created by aerofoil

Aerofoil

Direction of airflow

Above An aircraft wing in cross-section is shaped so that air has to travel further and faster over the top, sucking the wing upwards. At the same time, air passing under the wing pushes it upwards.

In straight, level flight, the lift generated by the wings is enough to carry the weight of an aircraft. Engine thrust more than compensates for drag, so the aircraft can move forward in the air.

Drag

Lift

G-WALND

Thrust

Weight of aircraft

An aircraft of simple construction has three basic sets of controls. A rudder on the tail, operated via cables by foot pedals in the cockpit, controls side-to-side movement, or yaw. Also on the tail plane are elevators, operated by to-and-fro movements of the pilot's control column. These control pitching, the up-and-down movement of the nose. Side-to-side movements of the control column operate ailerons on the wings, and these result in rolling movements of the aircraft.

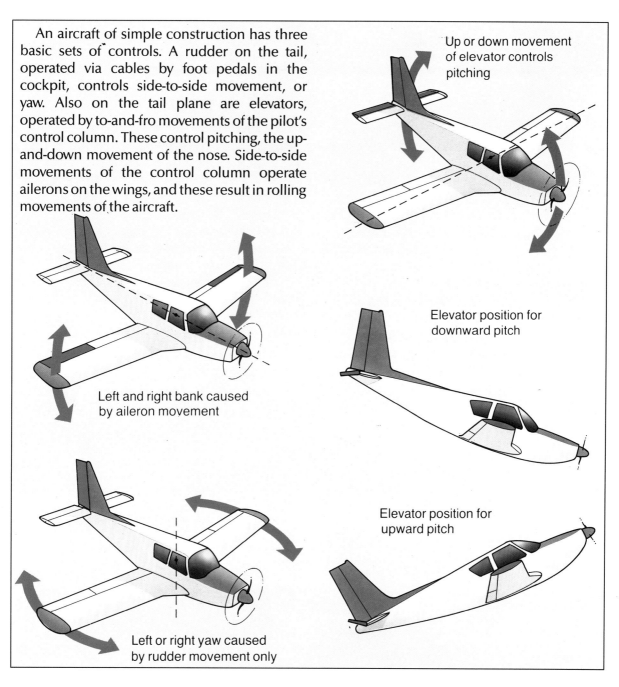

Up or down movement of elevator controls pitching

Elevator position for downward pitch

Elevator position for upward pitch

Left and right bank caused by aileron movement

Left or right yaw caused by rudder movement only

All these controls work by altering the lift characteristics of the surface to which they are attached. For example, lowering the elevators increases the curvature of the upper surface of the tailplane. As a result more lift is generated, the tailplane rises and the aeroplane starts to dive. Raising the elevators causes the aircraft to climb. The rudder acts in the same way to produce side-to-side movements of the aircraft. The ailerons act in opposition to each other. When one aileron is raised, the other is lowered, with the result that one wing drops while the other rises. By using the rudder at the same time, the aeroplane can be made to go into a banked turn Learner pilots need a lot of practice to do this smoothly.

Soon after the end of the First World War, pioneers began to show the world that long distance flights across oceans could be made in safety. The excitement of fast air travel soon became attractive to business people and the wealthy, and civil airlines opened up in a number of countries. The first passenger aircraft were biplanes, two-winged aeroplanes originally designed as wartime bombers, and often built of wood and fabric.

As more and more people wanted to travel by air, purpose-built passenger aeroplanes were developed to meet demand. Many of these were monoplanes, single-winged aircraft with two or three engines, and they made regular flights between the cities of Europe and those of the United States. During the 1930s, huge four-engined flying boats became popular for long distance flights across oceans, but they could only take off and land on calm water and were not as safe as people believed. They were also slow and costly to manufacture.

The giant Dornier Do-X flying boat of 1929 could carry 150 passengers and 10 crew. It was powered by twelve engines mounted in six pairs above the wing.

This Douglas Dakota was the R.A.F. version of the American Douglas C-47 Skytrain, developed from the DC-3. This was one of the first international airliners, carrying 32 passengers at about 270 kph. The DC-3 had a thin outer skin of polished aluminium. It was first flown in 1936 and by the end of the second World War over 10,000 of these aircraft had been built. A few are still flying.

The modern airliner was born in the mid-1930s with the arrival of the first of the all-metal low-wing monoplanes, the Boeing 247 and the Douglas DC-2. The DC-2, and later the DC-3, proved to be faster, more reliable and more economical to operate than any of its rivals. Carrying up to 32 passengers, this aircraft helped to make air travel cheaper, and, by 1939, nine out of every ten airliners in use throughout the world were DC-3s.

Before the Second World War and for a few years after it ended, airliners were powered by piston engines and their speed was limited. Their days were soon numbered by the arrival of the jet engine. The first turbojet airliner was the de Havilland DH 106 Comet, which was put into service in 1952. With its four wing-mounted jet engines, it had a cruising speed of about 800 kph, much faster than any other airliner of the time. The Comet is considered by many to be one of the most beautiful aircraft ever built, but unfortunately it was soon beset with problems. During 1953 and 1954 two Comets broke up in mid-air, killing everyone on board, and all Comets were grounded. Eventually, it was found that these accidents had been caused by weaknesses in the design of the cabin structure. In 1958 a redesigned version, the Comet 4, was put into service and remained in use until the 1970s. Since the introduction of the Comet, the basic design and appearance of the airliners have changed very little.

A modern 'jumbo', such as this Boeing 747-400, is an impressive sight.

The Comet was followed by the Boeing 707, the first of a long and highly successful family of aircraft. Other turbojets included the Douglas DC-8 and the Sud-Aviation Caravelle. The Caravelle had two engines mounted on the fuselage near the tail, allowing the wing to operate with greatest efficiency.

By now, all long range airliners were designed, like the Comet, to cruise at altitudes between 6,000 and 12,000 metres. At this height, not only is the air calmer, making flight more comfortable for the passengers, but the engines and wings can operate at the highest efficiency. Above a height of about 2,500 metres, the

The cockpit of a McDonnell Douglas DC-10, a wide-bodied aircraft that first saw service during the early 1970s. The crew of the aircraft consists of the pilot, co-pilot, and flight engineer.

pressure, of the atmosphere falls rapidly, and for passenger comfort the cabin has to be pressurized, and kept pumped up by electric motors to a pressure to which people are accustomed on the ground. This calls for an airtight cabin with a cross-section which is circular. Smaller passenger aircraft that do short journeys and cruise at lower heights can have fuselages that are box-shaped since the cabins do not need to be pressurized.

The more passengers an airliner can carry, the more economic it usually becomes, and the cheaper it is to fly. The year 1969 saw the first of the big wide-bodied jet airliners, the Boeing 747, which can carry between 320 and 500 passengers. It was followed by other wide-bodied airliners, such as the McDonnell Douglas DC-10, the Lockheed 1011 Tristar and the Airbus Industrie A300B.

Among the latest airliners is the wide-bodied Boeing 747-400. This has a fully computerized, digital cockpit that can be operated by a flying crew of two. A flight engineer is no longer needed, since engine performance is continually monitored by computer. It has advanced engines that consume less fuel and the aircraft can fly about 13,000 km without refuelling. All these factors help to reduce the cost of long-distance air travel.

Smaller airliners, such as the Boeing 757 and 767, are also equipped with digital cockpits. The Airbus A320 is equipped with the latest avionics and fly-by-wire systems (see page 34). Nearly all of this aircraft's functions are electronically controlled, involving over fifteen different interlinked computers. A centralized fault display system flashes up faults on a screen near the pilots. This system will soon be modified so that details of faults can be signalled to the ground. By the time the aircraft lands, ground engineers will have plans ready for repair work to begin immediately.

Supersonic flight

As an aircraft moves through the air, pressure waves move out in front of it. These travel at the speed of sound (about 1,220 kph). When the aircraft reaches the speed of sound, the pressure waves 'pile up' in front of it. The increase in pressure has the result of creating shock waves. These build up on various parts of the aircraft, including the leading and trailing edges of the wings.

In generating lift, the air above the wing travels faster than the aircraft itself. When the aircraft is travelling at very nearly the speed of sound, the air above the wing may actually be moving at a supersonic speed. The flow pattern of the air becomes more turbulent as the speed of sound is reached. Once the aircraft exceeds the speed of sound (Mach 1), it is said to pass through the sound barrier. The aircraft overtakes the pressure waves and the shock waves form a cone that spreads out behind it. As the shock waves pass over the ground below, a dull sonic boom is heard.

Right The Anglo-French Concorde is, at present, the only supersonic airliner in service.

All aircraft that fly at supersonic speeds are designed to pierce the pressure waves with the least amount of drag. The nose must be pointed and the wings have to be tapered. In appearance, a supersonic aircraft is shaped like a paper dart.

Military aircraft

The major roles of military aircraft were largely established in the First World War. These are reconnaissance, defending airspace and attacking ground targets, often deep into enemy territory. In warfare, both sides try to gain superiority over each other in the performance and capabilities of their aircraft. In times of peace, each nation tries to maintain an up-to-date air force that can carry out these roles should it be called upon to do so.

Keeping up-to-date and maintaining supremacy involves constant changes and improvements in design. Technology has moved so rapidly that the military aircraft of today bear little or no resemblance to the piston-engined fighters and bombers of the Second World War.

The main role of a modern jet fighter is to defend a country's airspace by intercepting and attacking hostile aircraft. Fighters intended primarily for air combat, such as the American General Dynamics F-16 Fighting Falcon are designed to engage in air combat with enemy fighters. Interceptors, such as the Soviet Mig-25, use long-range missiles to deal with intruders such as enemy bombers. However, most modern fighters are said to be multi-role. They can carry out a variety of roles. Examples include the Dassault-Breguet Mirage 2000, the Grumman F-14 Tomcat and the Panavia Tornado. Some fighter aircraft, such as the Vought A-7 Corsair II and the British Aerospace (Hawker Siddeley) Sea Harrier, are designed to operate from the decks of aircraft carriers.

A fighter is powered by one or two very powerful turbojet or turbofan engines. Afterburners (see glossary) provide bursts of extra power at take-off or in flight. The engines of some modern fighter aircraft are capable of generating enough thrust to achieve speeds of up to two and a half times the speed of sound, that is 2,660 kph, called Mach 2·5. Radar equipment in the nose cone of the aircraft is used to help locate enemy aircraft. Many fighters have electronic equipment for jamming enemy detection devices.

The modern jet fighter is a highly sophisticated flying machine. Other types of aircraft are steady and stable in the air, but the latest fighters are designed to be less stable, which makes them more manoeuvrable. A fighter of this type is kept stable automatically by computer systems and the pilot flies the aircraft using a fly-by-wire system. This is described on page 34.

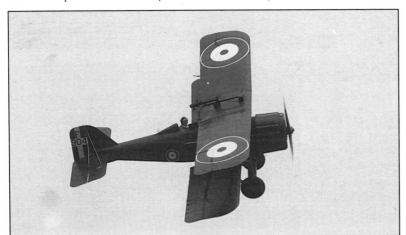

The Royal Aircraft Factory S.E. 5a was one of the most successful British fighters of the First World War. Powered by an 8-cylinder engine, it could reach speeds of over 220 kph. At the end of the war there were about 2,700 S.E. 5as in service with the Royal Air Force.

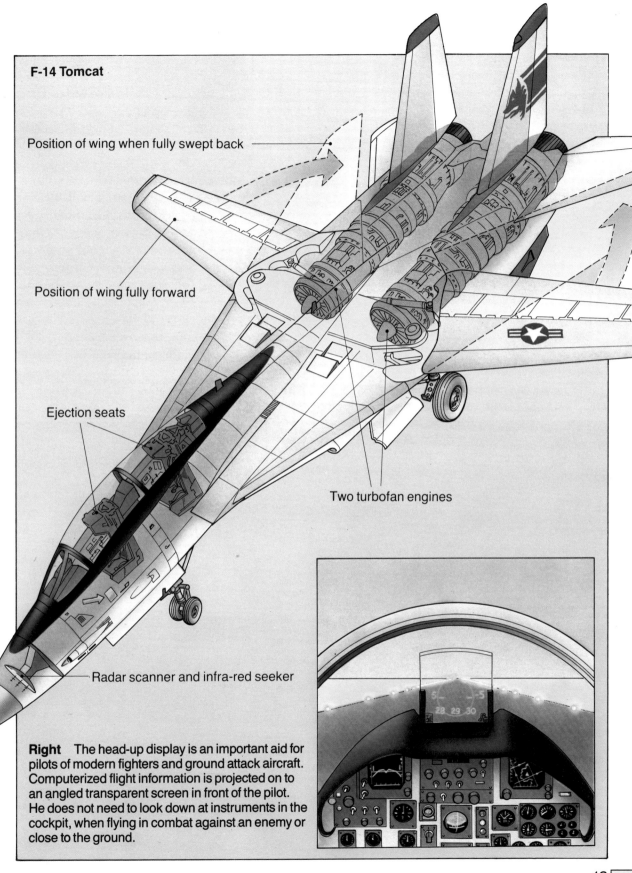

F-14 Tomcat

Position of wing when fully swept back

Position of wing fully forward

Ejection seats

Two turbofan engines

Radar scanner and infra-red seeker

Right The head-up display is an important aid for pilots of modern fighters and ground attack aircraft. Computerized flight information is projected on to an angled transparent screen in front of the pilot. He does not need to look down at instruments in the cockpit, when flying in combat against an enemy or close to the ground.

13

The task of attacking targets on the ground is generally carried out by bombers and specialized ground attack aircraft. Strategic bombers are large aircraft with long ranges and can operate deep inside enemy territory. Ground attack aircraft operate over battlefields or some way behind enemy front lines.

The modern strategic bomber can carry conventional bombs, free-fall nuclear bombs or nuclear missiles. Bombs have to be dropped over the target, whereas missiles can be released from some distance away. Air-launched cruise missiles can be released over 2,500 km from their targets. One of the longest-serving bombers is the Boeing B-52 Fortress, which first flew in the mid-1950s. It is now being replaced by the Rockwell B-1B, a swing-wing (see glossary) aircraft powered by four turbofan engines and equipped with the latest electronics. It has a guidance system that allows it to fly to its target at very low level so that it cannot be detected by enemy ground-based radar. Electronic counter measures (ECM) equipment allows the modern bomber to evade enemy detection equipment and missiles.

The modern attack, or close air support (CAS), aircraft is equipped with a similar range of electronic devices. The Grumman A-6 intruder can operate in any weather conditions. This and many other attack aircraft resemble large fighters and, indeed, fighters are sometimes used for attack missions. However, the use of heat-seeking missiles launched by an enemy from the ground has resulted in the development of specialized CAS aircraft, such as the Fairchild A-10A Thunderbolt. The engines

The Rockwell B1A bomber is designed for flying over enemy territory at low level. It is equipped with radar that enables the aircraft to fly close to the ground.

Guided missiles

Air-to-air infrared homing missile
This homes in on the heat produced by the target's engines.

Air-to-air radar-seeking missile
This is guided by the attacking aircraft's radar, which locks on to the target aircraft.

Air-to-ground laser-guided missile
This homes in on a spot of laser light on the target. The target is picked out by forces on the ground or by another control aircraft.

Air-to-ground television-guided missile
This uses a television seeker that is programmed by the pilot of the attacking aircraft. He uses a TV monitor in the cockpit.

Anti-ship missile
This has a guidance system that can be programmed with the target's distance and direction by the attacking aircraft. After launch, a navigation system in the missile guides it towards the target. Then, at about ten kilometres distance from the target, the missile switches on its own active radar seeker. This locks the missile on to the target. There is a built-in altimeter so that the missile can fly the last few kilometres just above the sea.

Air-launched cruise missile
The cruise missile finds its own way to a programmed target. It uses a guidance system that allows it to fly just above the ground, so as to avoid detection by enemy radar. An on-board computer has maps and other information stored in its memory. This is matched against a radar altimeter and an autopilot in the missile makes necessary changes in course.

Right A Panavia Tornado with the range of weapons it can carry. It is a multi-role aircraft, but its main tasks are to attack targets on the ground and to intercept enemy fighters and bomber aircraft. It has been designed to do the jobs of several different types of military aircraft.

of the A-10A are mounted high on the rear fuselage so that they are shielded against heat-seeking missiles from the ground by the wings and tailplane. The aircraft is armed with a seven-barrel 30mm cannon in the nose and carries missiles that are guided by television. Other ground attack aircraft are armed with bombs and missiles that are guided by infrared or laser techniques. Maritime attack aircraft carry torpedoes, cluster bombs, depth bombs and anti-ship missiles such as the Exocet missile, manufactured in France.

Other military aircraft also play important roles, particularly helicopters (see page 18) and transporters used for carrying troops to battle areas, or dropping them by parachute. Reconnaissance and intelligence gathering is also vital and the modern reconnaissance aircraft is equipped with sophisticated cameras, infrared sensors and radar. Maritime reconnaissance aircraft detect submarines with magnetic detectors, and they can even use sniffing devices that can detect the diesel fumes of enemy submarines.

All pilots need to learn their skills and it is often safest to learn on dual-control aircraft designed for training. Probably the most famous trainer in the history of flying is the de Havilland Tiger Moth. It ceased being used as a trainer after the Second World War, but is still flown by enthusiasts. Today, in Britain, fighter pilots begin their training on the new Shorts Tucano, a turboprop aircraft originally developed in Brazil. From this they progress to the British Aerospace Hawk T1. In the U.S.A., military pilots start their training in a Cessna T-37 or Fairchild Republic T-46A, before progressing to the Northrop T-38 Talon. In other parts of the world the SIAI Marchetti SF260 is often used to train both military and civil pilots.

Anyone can learn to fly, and a variety of light touring aircraft can be used for this purpose. Examples include the Cessna 150 series and the Scottish Aviation Beagle Pup. The Rheims-Cessna 152 is also used for aerobatic training, and there are a number of very specialized aerobatic display aircraft, such as the Pitts Special. Very rugged, basic aircraft are used in

HRH The Duchess of York seen at the controls of a small training aircraft. All beginners have to learn navigation techniques and how to use radio.

The Super Guppy is designed to carry large sections of other aircraft.

some countries for agricultural purposes, particularly crop spraying; the Ipanema, built in Brazil, is an example.

Larger aircraft can carry several passengers; examples include the Cessna Centurion and the Britten Norman Islander. Business travellers often need more rapid transport and the business jet was invented by the American, William Lear, in the 1960s. The Gates Learjets have been popular for many years and, in 1984, the Learfan was the first aircraft to be built mostly of advanced composite materials. The Beech Starship, with its pusher propellers and canard wing arrangement (see page 27), is based on a design by the American Bert Rutan. Today, the transport of cargo is still an important part of an airline's operations. Many freight- carrying aircraft are conversions of passenger aeroplanes; the Boeing 747-200F is an example. However, there are also specialized transport aircraft, such as the Super Guppy, which is used to transport Airbus sections from their assembly to the main production line in Toulouse in France. Large transports are also used for military purposes. Examples include the Lockheed C5 Galaxy and the C130 Hercules, which has been widely used in famine relief operations. The largest of all is the Soviet Antonov An-124, which can carry loads of up to about 150,000 kg.

The Lockheed Starlifter, seen here with an all-female crew, is a long-range transport aircraft.

The helicopter was originally developed from a machine known as the autogyro, invented in the early 1920s by a Spaniard, Juan de la Cierva. This used an unpowered, three-bladed rotor to provide an otherwise normal aeroplane with extra lift. The autogyro could not hover, but it could fly very slowly and land almost vertically. Encouraged by the success of Cierva's C-30 autogyro, several aircraft designers began work on machines that could hover, using powered rotors. In 1942, the first practical helicopter was developed by the American Igor Sikorsky.

The modern helicopter is very versatile. Many kinds are used for military purposes. They make useful reconnaissance aircraft and can be used to carry troops to places where they are needed. Some helicopters, such as the Westland Lynx 3, the Bell AH-IS Cobra and the Soviet Mil Mi-24 Hind are equipped with missiles, machine guns and cannon. They are used as tank-killers or gunships, and may even engage each other in aerial combat. Naval forces use several kinds of helicopter, such as the Westland Sea King and the Westland Navy Lynx, for such purposes as hunting mines, and locating and shadowing enemy ships and submarines.

Military helicopters are also used for search and rescue — important in peacetime as well as in war. The Aerospatiale HH-65A Dolphin is designed for night search and rescue. Helicopters can also be used for lifting heavy weights; large heavy lifters include the Boeing Vertol CH-47 Chinook, the CH-53E Super Stallion and the giant Soviet helicopter, the Mil Mi-26 Halo, which can lift 20 tonnes. Other uses of helicopters include ferrying passengers between airports and city centres, ambulance work, and supplying offshore oil platforms.

The Bell AH-1W Super Cobra is an attack helicopter or gunship. It is armed with 20 mm cannon and carries a number of missiles.

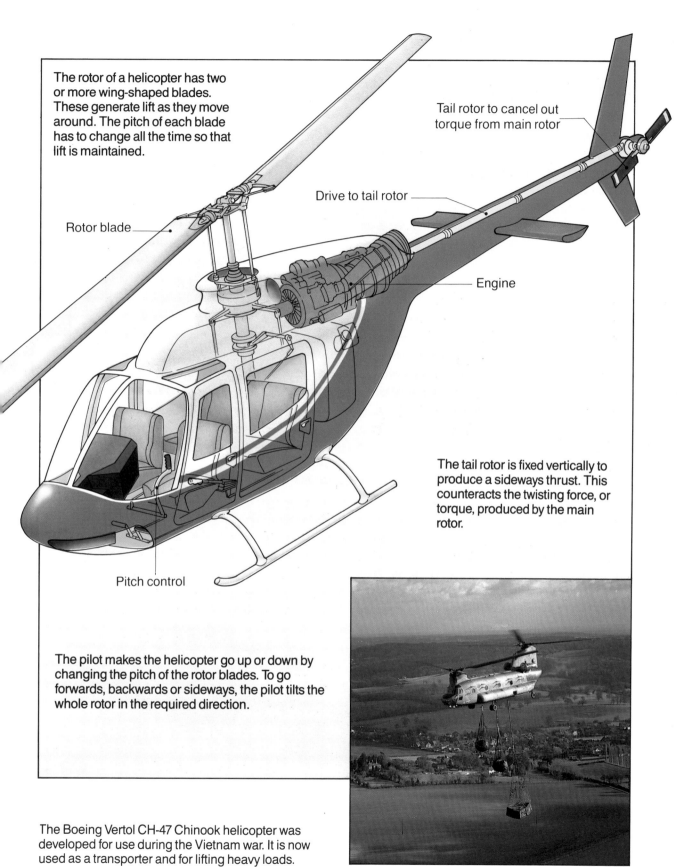

The rotor of a helicopter has two or more wing-shaped blades. These generate lift as they move around. The pitch of each blade has to change all the time so that lift is maintained.

Tail rotor to cancel out torque from main rotor

Drive to tail rotor

Rotor blade

Engine

The tail rotor is fixed vertically to produce a sideways thrust. This counteracts the twisting force, or torque, produced by the main rotor.

Pitch control

The pilot makes the helicopter go up or down by changing the pitch of the rotor blades. To go forwards, backwards or sideways, the pilot tilts the whole rotor in the required direction.

The Boeing Vertol CH-47 Chinook helicopter was developed for use during the Vietnam war. It is now used as a transporter and for lifting heavy loads.

There are many situations in which aircraft have to land and take off in a restricted space. Helicopters can often be used, but they are expensive to operate and lack the speed of winged aircraft. STOL (short take-off and landing) aircraft have evolved for use on small airstrips in underdeveloped parts of the world and on the short runways of modern urban airports. Their wings are specially designed to generate the maximum possible amount of lift while moving at low speeds. Examples include the passenger-carrying de Havilland Canada Dash-7 and the de Havilland Buffalo, which is used as a military airlifter.

VTOL (vertical take-off and landing) aircraft were first developed in the 1950s for use on aircraft carriers and in clearings near a battle area. Several methods of achieving vertical take-off have been tried, but the most successful is the system now known as vectored thrust, developed by Hawker in Britain. Four swivelling nozzles direct the hot gases from two engines either downwards or backwards to provide lift or forward thrust. This system is used in the Hawker-Siddeley Harrier, of which there are now a number of versions. The most recent is the McDonnell Douglas AV-8B Harrier II.

The only other VTOL aircraft in service is the Soviet Yakovlev Yak-36 Forger, of which only about twelve exist. This aircraft can take off only vertically, whereas the Harrier can, and usually does, use a short take-off run.

A British Aerospace BAe 146 landing at the London City Airport. This aircraft can land on short runways only 1,200 m long, and is the world's quietest airliner.

The Harrier, originally developed by Hawker Siddeley, is one of today's most versatile
aircraft. Here, one of the latest versions, a McDonnell Douglas 8B Harrier II, is seen
hovering above the deck of an aircraft carrier.

Among the many VTOL systems tried out
during the 1950s and 1960s were tilt-propeller
and tilt-wing aircraft. This type of aircraft takes
off like a helicopter, but cruises like a
conventional turboprop aeroplane. Most of the
early types flew successfully, but they were
heavy and mechanically very complicated and
the idea was abandoned. Today, however,
tiltrotor aircraft can be built using modern
lightweight materials and are now starting to
reappear. The latest is the Boeing Vertol V-22
Osprey, and by the year 1990 companies in

Europe and the USA hope to develop medium-
sized passenger-carrying tiltrotor aircraft.
Military versions will also be developed and, if
successful, this type of aircraft may replace the
large helicopter.

Alternatively, some companies are working
on another new design, known as the X-wing
convertiplane. This will look like a streamlined
helicopter, with a four-bladed rotor and a pair of
small wings. At low speeds the rotor will turn
normally, but for high-speed flight it will be
locked and its blades will act like wings.

The first stage in producing a new aeroplane is the design. This includes not only the overall shape of the aircraft but also the shape and position of each individual part, of which there may be thousands. Careful drawings are made and today much of the design work is done using computers.

The purpose of a proposed aircraft largely determines its size and capabilities, but aircraft designers are constantly trying to find ways of increasing efficiency and reducing costs. Materials are particularly important; most metals are heavy and designers are always looking for new lightweight materials. Among the strongest are the composites made by combining carbon fibres with epoxy resins. Carbon fibres can also be made into a material known as carbon-carbon, and scientists are working on ways of mixing them with metals. Other important materials include amazingly tough synthetics, such as Kevlar and Nomex, and a new metal alloy of aluminium and lithium.

Before any construction is begun, models of the design are tested in a wind tunnel. Examples of the individual parts are made and each part is tested to destruction. For example, wires are attached to the wings, which are then bent until they break. Engines are made to run at full power until they fail. When all the parts have been tested a single prototype aircraft is built, and then test-flying begins.

When everything has been thoroughly tested, the aircraft enters the manufacturing stage. The building process is like a pyramid. At the base of the pyramid small parts are built into larger assemblies and systems. These are then taken away and combined with others to form still larger structures, and so on until the whole aircraft is complete.

Below A typical airliner final assembly line.

An assembly line making Grumman A-6F Intruders.

Simple equipment can be assembled in one place. More complex items may be assembled on a moving production line. Some kinds of delicate equipment are very sensitive to contamination by particles of dust. These have to be assembled in a 'clean room', from which all dust is carefully excluded.

The final assembly stages generally take place in a large hall, in which several aircraft can be built at the same time. First, the fuselage, including the cockpit and tail sections, is assembled from the two to five (depending on the type and size of aircraft) sub-assemblies already built. The wings are then added and the aircraft is fitted with its engines, flying systems and any necessary furnishings.

23

As air flows over a wing, the air nearest the surface is considerably slowed down by friction with the wing material. As a result, fast moving layers of air flow over slower layers near the wing. If this flow pattern is smooth, the airflow in the boundary layer (the layer next to the wing) is described as being laminar; if it is not, the airflow is described as turbulent.

A turbulent airflow always has the result of increasing drag, so wings have a smooth skin to keep this to a minimum. A typical wing generally produces laminar flow near the leading edge, but more turbulent flow farther back. Many modern aircraft have leading edge slats and slots to help control the boundary layer. Small protruding pieces of metal on the surface of the wing are sometimes used to help keep the boundary layer from separating away from the wing.

The amount of lift generated by a wing depends partly on its camber, or curvature. The camber can be temporarily increased by movable flaps on the leading and trailing edges on the wing. Moving the flaps downwards increases the airflow over the upper surface and thus increases the lift. At the same time they also increase drag, and flaps are therefore used during landing to reduce speed.

During landing, an aircraft needs to be travelling as slowly as possible while still maintaining enough lift to keep it in the air. To achieve this, the flaps are lowered and this maintains lift in the final stages of landing.

The effect of a flap can be increased by using high pressure air taken from the jet engines. Blowing this air through a row of ducts just in front of the flap forces the airflow down on to the flap and increases lift dramatically. A number of modern STOL aircraft (see page 20) use this method. Another method currently being developed is known as upper surface blowing. Instead of being vented behind the aircraft in the usual way, air from the jet engine exhaust is directed over flaps that curve sharply downwards. This speeds up the airflow over the wing, and a large part of the exhaust stream is directed almost downwards, thus greatly increasing lift during take-off or landing.

An idea currently being studied for high-speed aircraft is the mission adaptive wing (MAW), a flexible wing made of composite materials. The smooth surface will have no flaps, slats or spoilers to break up the airflow, and electronic controls will constantly adapt its shape to ensure that the aircraft flies as efficiently as possible at any speed and altitude.

Above A high-speed attack aircraft landing with its airbrakes fully extended. The extra drag created by these surfaces helps to slow the aircraft rapidly after touching down.

Wing construction

The wings of an aircraft are designed to be both as light and as strong as possible. Most aircraft have wings formed from a row of ribs, each shaped like an aerofoil. The ribs are linked by spars and the whole wing is covered with an outer skin of thin sheet metal. Light, strong metals are used.

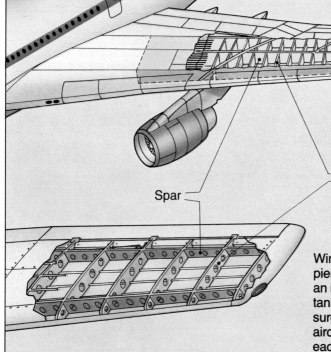

Spar

Ribs with aerofoil shape

Wings are basically hollow and the spars are pierced with many holes. A wing therefore makes an ideal place to store fuel. Many aircraft have fuel tanks built into the wings. Baffles stop the fuel from surging along the wing. The balance, or trim, of the aircraft is maintained by ensuring that tanks on each side contain the same amount of fuel.

The most efficient aircraft travel at fairly low speeds and tend to have long thin wings. Extreme examples of this type of wing can be seen in gliders and certain man-powered aircraft. At high speeds, however, such wings create too much drag. The wings of high-speed aircraft are therefore shorter and broader, and are often angled backwards.

Aircraft that fly faster than the speed of sound have special requirements because of the shock waves that build up on the leading and trailing edges of the wings. These shock waves produce extra drag, which can be reduced by having sharply pointed leading and trailing edges and thin, swept wings. Some modern supersonic aircraft have variable geometry, or swing-wings.

These can be swung forwards for take-off and low speed flight, and then swung back to reduce drag and allow the aircraft to fly at supersonic speeds.

Not all high-speed aircraft have swept wings. Some very fast aircraft have little or no sweep and others, such as the experimental Grumman X-29, have forward-swept wings, which provide excellent lift and manoeuvrability. Another new idea, being developed in the USA, is to have a pair of conventional swept wings joined to forward swept rear wings, producing a diamond-shaped silhouette.

The ultimate shape, perhaps, is the wingless aircraft, in which the fuselage itself is used to generate lift. Flying wings and wingless aircraft

A Grumman EF-111A Raven. Its swing wings enable it to fly efficiently both at subsonic and supersonic speeds.

The Beech Starship is one of the most exciting of today's aircraft. Its unusual design includes a canard wing arrangement, with a small foreplane in front of the main wing. Power is provided by pusher turboprop engines, and their efficiency is greatly increased by the use of winglets. These reduce drag by breaking up the vortices (spiral air currents) that tend to form behind the tips of wings.

are among those being investigated for the design concept known as stealth. The aim of stealth is to create military aircraft that are almost impossible to detect using radar or infrared. Such aircraft will have narrow profiles and no vertical surfaces to reflect radar signals. In addition, their paint will confuse radar signals and they will be constructed mostly of composite and plastic materials. These either reflect radar signals poorly or actually absorb them, making it difficult to detect the aircraft.

Among the latest aircraft designs is the canard wing arrangement, in which, instead of a tailplane, there is a small foreplane in front of the main wings. The Wright brothers' *Wright Flyer I* was a canard aircraft, but although the configuration has several advantages, it was abandoned on later aircraft because of stability problems. Using modern design techniques and electronics, such problems can now be overcome. In propeller-driven aircraft, the canard design has also allowed the use of pusher propellers, which are more efficient than tractor (puller) propellers.

Aircraft and the internal combustion engine developed at much the same time. In 1903, the *Wright Flyer I* was powered by a four cylinder, water cooled, 12 horsepower engine, designed by the Wright brothers themselves. It was an in-line engine with a single row of cylinders arranged along a rotating crankshaft that drove the propeller. Within a few years, other types of piston engines started to appear. In a V engine the cylinders are arranged in two rows, in order to reduce the overall length of the engine. A radial air-cooled engine consists of a ring of cylinders around the crankshaft. In a rotary engine the crankshaft is fixed and the cylinders themselves rotate. These carry the propeller with them.

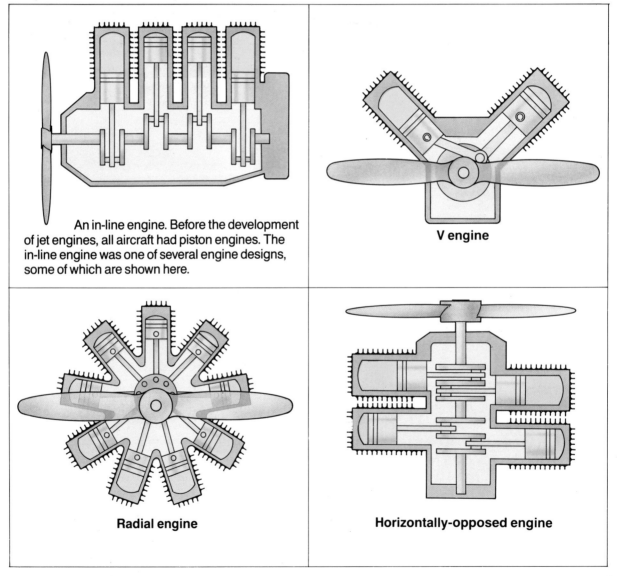

An in-line engine. Before the development of jet engines, all aircraft had piston engines. The in-line engine was one of several engine designs, some of which are shown here.

V engine

Radial engine

Horizontally-opposed engine

The Supermarine Spitfire, one of the most famous fighters of the Second World War, is powered by a Rolls Royce Merlin 12-cylinder, liquid-cooled engine. Over 20,300 Spitfires were built, more than any other British aeroplane.

Rotary engines were used in many First World War fighters. After the war, however, they were rapidly outdated by the new, more powerful radial, in-line and V engines. These engines reached their peak of development at the end of the Second World War. One leading engine was the Pratt and Whitney R-2800 Double Wasp, an 18-cylinder radial engine of up to 2,800 horsepower that is still in use today. Most of the piston engines developed since 1945 are flat-four or flat-six engines. In these engines, the cylinders are horizontally opposed.

In large aircraft, the piston engine driving a propeller has largely given way to the jet engine. In 1928 Frank Whittle, a young British pilot officer, was the first to suggest using a gas turbine engine to produce a jet of hot gases that would propel an aircraft. By 1937 he had built a prototype engine, which in 1941 powered the experimental Gloster E.28/39. Meanwhile, in Germany, Hans von Ohain had also been working on jet engines. The first jet aircraft to fly was the Heinkel He 178 in 1939. The first British jet fighter, the Gloster Meteor, took to the air in 1943, and the German Messerschmitt Me 262 first flew in 1944.

The first jet engines were of the type known as turbojets. Air enters the front of the engine through a compressor. Compressing the air heats it up and the hot compressed air then enters the combustion chambers, where fuel vapour is sprayed into it. The fuel ignites and the hot burning gases expand rapidly forcing their way out of the jet pipe at the rear of the engine. The gases pass through a turbine, which drives the compressor.

Jet engines use two main types of compressor. A centrifugal compressor is basically a spinning disc with built-in vanes. The air is flung outwards by the vanes and leaves the outside of the disc at high speed. As the air slows down, it is compressed.

An axial compressor consists of many sets of curved blades rotating between sets of fixed blades inside a tight-fitting casing. As the air passes through each set of blades it becomes more and more compressed. Centrifugal compressors are simpler and less easily damaged than axial compressors and were used a great deal in early jet aircraft. However, they have a much larger frontal area and cannot be used in supersonic aircraft. In addition, modern axial compressors can compress air up to 30 times normal air pressure, whereas most centrifugal compressors achieve no more than five to nine times normal air pressure.

The turbojet is suited to achieving high speeds. However, at low speeds it is inefficient, which makes it unsuitable for slower aircraft. The solution to this is to make the engine accelerate a greater amount of air more slowly. One way of doing this is to link a propeller, via a system of gears, to the turbine.

Today, turboprop engines are mostly used on smaller aircraft. On large airliners they have been superseded by another type of jet engine, known as the turbofan. In this type of engine, a greater airflow is generated by placing a large, low pressure compressor at the front of the engine. Some of the compressed air passes through the core of the engine in the normal way, but the remainder passes over the core through the rear of the engine. This has the advantage of making the engine much quieter.

Among the latest jets being developed are unducted fan (UDF) and high-speed turboprop engines, sometimes known as propfans. These are like turbofan engines with the outer cowling removed to save weight. The simplest type of propfan looks like a many-bladed turboprop engine. Another type being investigated by some aircraft manufacturers has two fans spinning in opposite directions. This engine could result in fuel savings of 30 per cent.

A Vickers Viscount, powered by four Rolls Royce Dart turboprop engines.

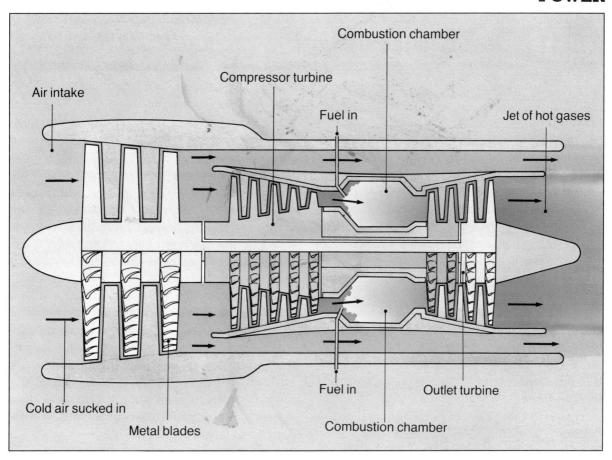

Air intake

Compressor turbine

Combustion chamber

Fuel in

Jet of hot gases

Cold air sucked in

Metal blades

Fuel in

Combustion chamber

Outlet turbine

Above A turbofan engine. Air drawn in by the metal blades of the fan is packed tight by a compressor turbine. Fuel is injected into the hot compressed air and burns fiercely. The hot expanding gases pass through the outlet turbine at the rear, and the powerful jet provides thrust.

Right A Boeing 747 is powered by four vast turbofan engines. Rolls Royce, Pratt & Whitney or General Electric engines are used.

Maintaining control of an aircraft requires constant vigilance on the part of a human pilot. In many aircraft, however, the task is aided by a mechanical automatic pilot, or autopilot. The first autopilots were devised in the 1920s to keep aircraft flying straight and level. Deviations were detected by gyroscopes and electrical or hydraulic signals were sent to small power units linked to the control surface mechanisms. By 1939, autopilots could undertake more complicated movements such as banked turns, and during the Second World War an autopilot could fly an aircraft on a specified compass heading at a particular speed and height. Today, an aircraft autopilot forms part of a modern flight-control system (FCS), which is controlled by computer.

The FCS also incorporates the navigation systems of each aircraft. Modern navigation systems use gyroscopes and other instruments to chart an aircraft's distance and direction from a known point.

Many of the navigation systems available are based on radio. Automatic direction finding (ADF) systems, such as Omega, Decca and Loran, use signals beamed from ground-based radio stations. Aircraft can follow radio tracks produced by VOR (VHF-omnidirectional radio range) stations, calculating distance using distance measuring equipment (DME). VOR is often used together with inertial navigation to fly along a series of programmed waypoints. Increasingly, aircraft are using radio signals from satellites to pinpoint their position. At airports, instrument landing systems (ILS) use radio beacons to assist aircraft landing in poor visibility, and certain types of aircraft may be allowed to land in zero visibility.

From high in the control tower, air traffic controllers can see all of the airport. Radar screens enable them to keep track of all aircraft movements.

Whether on the ground or in the air, pilots use radio to keep in touch with the nearest control tower. Good radio communication systems and skills are essential.

Safety in the air is vital. In order to prevent collisions, there are strict rules governing how and where aircraft may fly. In most countries, every aircraft that takes off must have a flight plan, indicating exactly where it is going and how long the journey is expected to take. At all times the position of every aircraft is monitored on the radar screens of the local air traffic control station.

However, the world's air space is becoming more crowded, particularly near airports. Computer systems used for air traffic control are not yet as up-to-date as those on board many aircraft and neighbouring countries do not necessarily use matching systems. As a result near misses and accidents do happen.

A rotating radar aerial sends out a beam of radio signals. Signals reflected back from aircraft are received by the same aerial and appear on a screen similar to that of a television. Aircraft are shown as moving 'blips' of light.

Until recently the control surfaces of all aircraft were controlled by cables or hydraulic fluids in pipes. However, the science of microelectronics has begun to revolutionize aircraft design and in the modern computerized aircraft, the mechanical links from the control column are being replaced by electrical wires. In this system, known as fly-by-wire, movements of the control column generate electrical signals, which are fed to the computer. This interprets the signals and sends its own digital instructions to servo motors linked directly to the control surfaces.

The pilot still appears to control the aircraft in the normal way, using a control column or, as in the Airbus A.320, a small side-stick control. But because the pilot's controls are no longer directly linked to the control surfaces, the pilot can no longer feel the response of these surfaces. In order to compensate for this, designers sometimes incorporate 'feel' directly into the pilot's controls.

Electrical wires are lighter than mechanical control devices and are easier to install in aircraft. In the latest aircraft, instead of each instrument and control having its own pair of wires, a number of systems are linked on a single set of wires thus saving weight.

The digital cockpit of a Boeing 747-400. The layout is similar to the cockpit of the Airbus A.320, but the Boeing is fitted with a normal control column.

Fly-by-wire

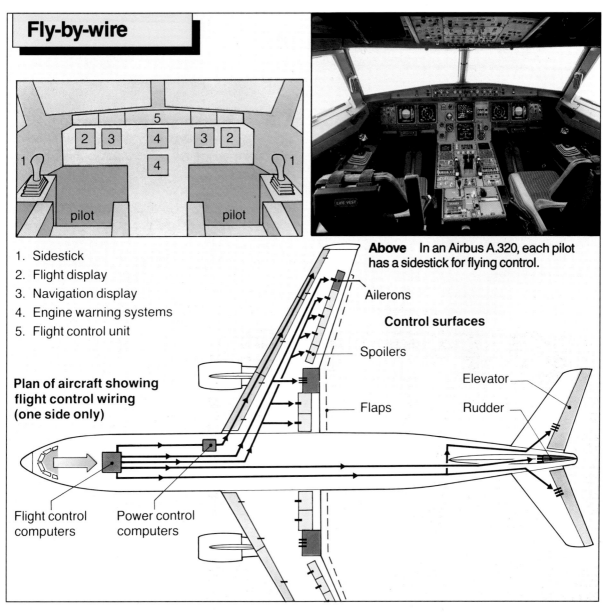

1. Sidestick
2. Flight display
3. Navigation display
4. Engine warning systems
5. Flight control unit

Above In an Airbus A.320, each pilot has a sidestick for flying control.

Plan of aircraft showing flight control wiring (one side only)

Flight control computers

Power control computers

Ailerons

Control surfaces

Spoilers

Flaps

Elevator

Rudder

The aircraft computer can also operate other controls, such as the engine throttles. It can receive information from the aircraft's monitoring devices, such as temperature gauges, airspeed indicator, altitude, attitude and rate of climb sensors, and this has enabled the cockpit layout to be greatly simplified. Instead of switches, the digital cockpit uses push-button controls.

Instead of a vast array of confusing dials, the latest digital cockpits have just a few, easily read digital displays. Each one resembles a small television screen and can show several different types of information. The A.320 Airbus, for example, has four main displays. Each pilot has a flight display, which shows altitude, artificial horizon and other information, and a navigation display, on which can be shown such things as the flight plan, navigation beacons and information from the inertial navigation system. The two other main displays show other flight information and engine data, and in addition there are a pair of screens that form part of the aircraft's centralized fault display system.

Modern aircraft are costly to build and expensive to operate. So pilot training is often carried out in an aircraft simulator - a machine that mimics very realistically the conditions on board a real aircraft. Using such a simulator, examiners can test a pilot's knowledge and skill to the limit, but without putting either people or aircraft at any kind of risk. Even if the pilot 'crashes' the simulator, he can walk away unharmed, if a little red in the face!

As might be expected, at the heart of a modern flight simulator is a computer. Each

simulator is designed to simulate a particular aircraft and the computer is programmed with all the aircraft's flight behaviour under any of the conditions the real aircraft might encounter. The pilot sits in a realistic reconstruction of the aircraft cockpit, in which are all the controls and instruments that would normally be present. Using the controls, the pilot makes the simulator go through all normal aircraft manoeuvres, such as take-off and landing, while the simulator controllers can add a wide range of unexpected events. The results of what the

Left An outside view of an Airbus A.300 flight simulator. Inside the simulator, all movements of the controls made by the pilot result in movement of the hydraulic rams. This makes the cabin move, like an aircraft in flight.

In this F-18 Hornet simulator, the pilot sees two hostile aircraft before him.

pilot does are fed back to the instruments in the simulator. Looking through the windscreen, the pilot sees a film sequence of the outside world. Several projectors, under the control of the main computer, project realistic images (generated by another computer) on to a wide screen in front of the pilot. This shows such things as a runway or other aircraft.

From the outside, the simulator can be seen for what it really is – a box of sophisticated electronics, linked to powerful computers and mounted on several hydraulic rams. Operated by a motion system control computer (under the direction of the main computer), a hydraulic power unit makes the rams move up and down in such a way that the pilot above actually feels the movements of the 'aircraft'.

Simulators are mainly used to help experienced military and airline pilots learn the techniques necessary to fly aircraft that are new to them. Normally, this would require many hours flying time, but the hours spent in the air can be greatly reduced by the use of a simulator. In time, perhaps, all such training will take place in a simulator. Civil pilots are more concerned with making sure that they know how to fly a new aircraft safely. Military pilots, on the other hand, can 'attack' computer-generated targets on the ground or engage in make-believe 'combat' with 'enemy aircraft'.

Long before the Wright brothers took to the air in a heavier-than-air craft, people had been taking off in craft that rose up because they were lighter than the air around them. The Montgolfier brothers ascended in their first hot air balloon in 1783 and in the same year the first gas balloon, filled with hydrogen, was devised by Professor Jacques Charles. The first airships were created by adding engines to balloons and airships were used by both sides during the First World War.

After the war, airship travel became popular, and huge airships carried passengers across the Atlantic. However, several disastrous crashes during the 1930s brought an end to the development of these large, hydrogen-filled airships. By the 1970s the only airships in

existence were a small fleet of airships kept by Goodyear for publicity purposes.

Today, airship designers see many possible roles for airships, including aerial survey work, pollution monitoring, fertilizer spreading and forestry. Instead of highly flammable hydrogen gas, they are filled with the non-flammable hydrogen gas, they are filled with the non-flammable gas helium, a by-product of the oil and nuclear industries. At the same time there are new lightweight metal alloys, plastics and composite materials available for constructing airships. One of today's most advanced airships is Airship Industries Skyship 500, which has a gondola made of Kevlar and glass fibre. It is driven by two vectored thrust fan propellers, and is highly manoeuvrable.

In the future, giant megalifters could transport goods in large containers.

Right Hot air balloons in flight. The technology has changed little over the centuries.

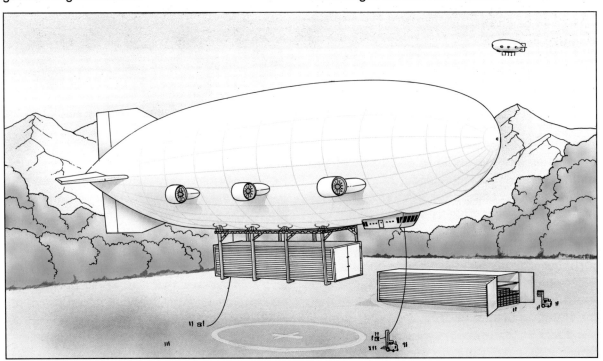

Airships have large amounts of available space and could operate using bulky but cheap fuels like natural gas or liquid hydrogen. They could be capable of enormous lifting power, particularly if combined with wings or rotors. Several designs for megalifters and aerial cranes have been suggested.

Gas-filled balloons are still used for scientific purposes, such as studying the weather. Modern materials and technology have also enabled balloon enthusiasts to develop a new version of the first aerial craft, the hot air balloon. The modern hot air balloon now carries its own source of heat, in the form of propane gas burners, and can therefore travel much further than Montgolfier's balloons. The envelope of a hot air balloon is generally made of nylon coated with polyurethane, but manufacturers have been experimenting with Kevlar, a very tough, heat-resistant fabric.

On gossamer wings

Orville and Wilbur Wright were originally glider pilots. Their knowledge of aircraft came from flying unpowered gliders, and they had benefited from the work of earlier glider pioneers, such as Sir George Cayley, Otto Lilienthal and Octave Chanute. Today, the challenge and thrill of flying unpowered aircraft remains the same and there are glider enthusiasts all over the world.

The modern glider resembles a conventional powered aircraft. However, there is no engine to generate thrust and forward movement is produced by a combination of the downward pull of the aircraft's weight and the lift generated by the wings. Thus a glider is built of light materials, and its long, thin wings and narrow fuselage are designed to increase lift and reduce drag. The pilot keeps the glider airborne by using upcurrents of air, and in this way can fly considerable distances.

Another form of glider that has become popular recently is the hang-glider. This is simply an aerofoil, created by stretching fabric across a frame, under which is suspended the pilot. The modern hang-glider resembles the gliders used by Lilienthal in the 1890s and is controlled in the same way, by body movements of the pilot. A microlight is basically a hang-glider equipped with an engine, although some microlights have rigid wings and a pilot's seat.

Microlights are very small aircraft with wings like those of a hang glider. This AB 'Scout' has a very small petrol engine and a flimsy seat for the pilot.

In 1986, Americans Dick Rutan and Janet Yeager flew their aircraft *Voyager* around the world without refuelling.

Almost everything that has not been achieved is regarded by someone as a challenge, and the man-powered aircraft is no exception. In 1977, *Gossamer Condor* designed by Dr Paul MacCready and Peter Lissaman, won the £50,000 Kremer Prize for being the first man-powered aircraft to fly over more than 1.6km (one mile). In 1979 its successor *Gossamer Albatross* was pedal-propelled 37km across the English Channel by the American racing cyclist Bryan Allen. Paul MacCready went on to design *Solar Challenger*, which crossed the English Channel in 1981. It was powered by 16,000 solar cells mounted on the upper surfaces of the wings and tailplane. In the future, if solar cells can be made more efficient, solar-powered aircraft may become more common.

One of the latest challenges to have been undertaken is that of flying an aircraft around the world without refuelling. This was achieved in 1986 by the aircraft *Voyager*, flown by the Americans Dick Rutan and Janet Yeager. The aircraft, made almost entirely of lightweight composites, carried over three times its own weight of fuel and was little more than a flying fuel tank. The journey took just under 13 days.

◁ 16 ▷ Tomorrow's aircraft

Many different types of possible future aircraft are already technically feasible. What remains to be seen is which of them are needed by the flying public and which ones can be produced and operated economically. The price and availability of fuel may become an increasingly important factor and some future aircraft may be fuelled by liquid hydrogen.

Large subsonic passenger aircraft will probably not change much in outward appearance, although Lockheed have proposed an airliner that has a huge ring wing arching upwards from the sides of the aircraft. However, the numbers of passengers are increasing on some routes and it therefore seems likely that the next generation of wide-bodied aircraft will be even larger than those of today, carrying perhaps 700 passengers on each flight. Propfan engines, one of the most promising modern developments, may help to keep down fuel costs. Another possibility is that of linking two large aircraft bodies under a single wing. Lockheed have suggested joining two C-5 Galaxies to form a double jumbo.

The Lockheed proposal for an advanced supersonic transport. This would carry 290 passengers over 7,400 km, and would travel at 2½ times the speed of sound.

This transport aircraft, also proposed by Lockheed, would be efficient at subsonic and supersonic speeds. Above the atmosphere it would fly at Mach 30.

For long-distance travel many people consider that supersonic flight will become more widespread, as the prospect of travelling half-way round the world in just a few hours appeals to more people. A supersonic transport could be powered by engines that operate like conventional turbofans at low speeds but like turbojets at supersonic speeds. Achieving near perfect laminar flow control is highly desirable, and McDonnell Douglas have designed a wing that has a smooth titanium skin perforated by millions of tiny pores. Air drawn through the pores holds the boundary layer on to the wing.

Alternatively, the high speed air transports of the future may be very fast space planes, such as the British Hotol and the American Orient Express, currently being developed. Powered by rocket engines that can use ordinary air at low levels, such planes will climb to around 100km and reach speeds of around Mach 20. They will thus be capable of flying half-way round the world in less than an hour, an idea that would have seemed impossible to the Wright brothers who made the first powered flight in 1903. Since the beginning of the 20th century, aircraft technology has made tremendous advances.

Glossary

Afterburner. The chamber in the tail pipe of a turbojet or turbofan engine in which fuel vapour is injected into the hot gases. The fuel ignites and gives extra thrust. Afterburners are generally found in fighters and are used for take-off and in combat.

Ailerons. Control surfaces on the trailing edge of an aircraft's wings that are used to bank the aircraft in a turn. Delta-winged aircraft have elevons, which are combined elevators and ailerons.

Avionics. Aviation electronics. An aircraft's electronic control and sensing equipment.

Biplane. An aircraft with two pairs of wings, one pair placed above the other.

Camber. The curvature of the upper surface of the wing.

Canard. A wing arrangement in which, instead of a tailplane being present, a small foreplane is placed in front of the main wing.

CAS. Close air support. A ground attack aircraft designed to support troops and armoured vehicles on a battlefield.

Composite. A material made up of two or more different materials, such as fibreglass and epoxy resin, or carbon fibre and epoxy resin.

Digital. Concerned with numbers, or digits. Digital computers store information and send signals in the form of codes that represent numbers.

Drag. The rearward-directed force on an aircraft created by the resistance of the air to its passage.

ECM. Electronic countermeasures. Electronic devices used to jam or mislead enemy radar.

Elevators. Control surfaces on the rear of an aircraft's tailplane that are used to make the aircraft climb or dive.

Flap. Small aerofoil on either the leading or trailing edge of a wing, used to generate extra lift by increasing the camber of the wing.

Fly-by-light. A system in which a pilot controls an aircraft by means of light signals travelling along optical fibres.

Fly-by-wire. A system in which a pilot controls an aircraft by means of electronic signals that travel along electrical wires, rather than mechanical linkages.

Head-up display. A device in an aircraft cockpit that projects computerized information from the instruments into a transparent screen in front of the pilot's line of sight.

Inertial guidance. A system in an aircraft or missile that uses inertial navigation equipment linked to the flight controls, in order to guide the craft to a pre-programmed destination.

Inertial navigation. A system in an aircraft or missile that uses a computer linked to gyroscopes and other instruments to calculate the aircraft's position in relation to a known starting point.

Jet engine. An internal combustion engine in which fuel vapour mixed with compressed air is burned continuously in combustion chambers to produce a jet of hot expanding exhaust gases.

Lift. The upward force generated by the wing of an aeroplane, the rotor of a helicopter, or the downwardly-directed jets of a VTOL aircraft.

MAW. Mission adaptive wing. A wing whose aerodynamic profile can be continually adjusted in flight to suit the aircraft's speed and height under any conditions.

Monoplane. An aircraft with a single pair of wings attached to the fuselage.

Piston engine. An internal combustion engine in which fuel vapour mixed with compressed air is burned explosively in cylinders. The burning fuel mixture expands and drives pistons linked to a rotating crankshaft.

Radar. Radio direction and ranging. A method of using radio waves to locate the direction and distance of an object. The position of the object is generally indicated on a television-like screen.

Stealth. The design used for military aircraft in which the aircraft is almost impossible to detect by radar or infrared.

STOL. Short take-off and landing. Some aircraft use STOVL, short take-off and vertical landing.

Strategic bomber. A military aircraft flown deep inside enemy territory during a war, and used to attack targets that are considered to be of importance.

Supersonic. Faster than the speed of sound.

Swing-wing. Variable geometry. A wing arrangement in which part or all of the wing can be moved forwards and outwards for subsonic flight and then swept back as the aircraft reaches supersonic speeds.

Thrust. The force created by an aircraft's propeller or jet. Thrust produces forward movement.

Turbofan. A jet engine in which a large low-pressure compressor, or fan, at the front of the engine is used to generate part of the thrust.

Turbojet. A jet engine in which all of the thrust is generated by the expulsion of the exhaust gases at the rear of the engine.

Vectored thrust. A system used in VTOL aircraft, in which the exhaust gases from the engines are directed in the required direction by swivelling nozzles.

VTOL. Vertical take-off and landing.

Further reading

Beaver P. (Ed), *The Encyclopedia of Aviation* (Octopus, 1986)

Cawthorne N., *Airliner* (Gloucester Press, 1987)

Ladd J.D., *Helicopters,* Modern Military Techniques (Dragon Grafton Books, 1986)

Lowe M., *Bombers,* Modern Military Techniques (Dragon Grafton Books, 1986)

Lowe M., *Fighters,* Modern Military Techniques (Dragon Grafton Books, 1986)

Mondey D. (Ed), *International Encyclopedia of Aviation* (Octopus, 1977)

Sweetman B., *Aircraft 2000* (Hamlyn, 1984)

Picture Acknowledgements

The publishers would like to thank the following for allowing their photographs to be reproduced in this book: AMD-BA/Aviaplans cover; Aviation Photographs International 15, 17 (below), 19, 29, 30, 33 (left); BAA Gatwick 5 (below); BBC Hulton Picture Library 8, 9; Boeing Commercial Airplane Company 10 (above), 34; Camera Press 16; Quadrant Picture Library 14, 23, 41; Rex Features 11; Spectrum Colour Library 40; Topham 5 (above), 10 (below), 31, 33 (right); TRH 12, 17 (above), 18, 20, 21, 25, 26, 27, 35, 36, 37, 42, 43; ZEFA 22, 24, 32, 39. Artwork by Nick Hawken.

Index